Text copyright © 2023 Karen Rosario Ingerslev

Illustrations copyright © 2023 Jennifer Davison

This edition copyright © 2023 Lion Hudson IP Limited

Published by **Lion Children's Books**

www.lionhudson.com

Part of the SPCK Group

SPCK, 36 Causton Street, London, SW1P 4ST

ISBN 978-0-7459-9801-5

First edition 2023

A catalogue record for this book is available from the British Library

Produced on paper from sustainable sources

Printed and bound in China, July 2023 by Dream Colour (Hong Kong) Printing Limited

Numbers
A Nativity Story

Words by
Karen Rosario Ingerslev
Pictures by
Jennifer Davison

LION
CHILDREN'S

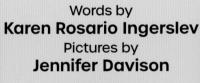

1 one

One special baby
asleep in the hay.

2 two

Two proud parents
watch and pray.

3 three

Three wise men
carry treats.

4 four

Four old camels
have hairy feet.

5 five

Five brown cows
stand on a hill.

five 5

6 six

Six tired shepherds keep very still.

six 6

7 **seven**

Seven holy angels
sing a song.

seven 7

8 eight

Eight happy sheep
dance along.

eight 8

9 nine

Nine busy inns
locked up tight.

nine 9

10 ten

Ten twinkling stars shine very bright.

ten 10

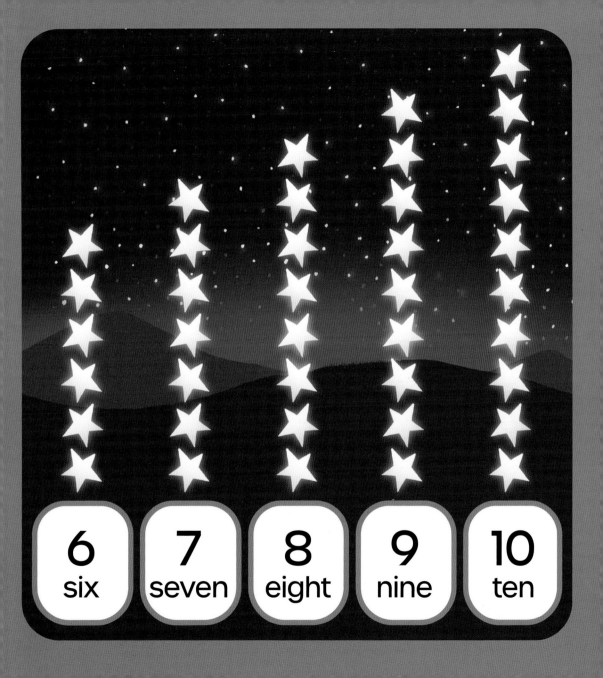

ALSO IN THE

Share a Story **BIBLE** *Buddies*

SERIES

Colours: A Noah's Ark Story

ISBN 978-0-7459-9802-2